YOU CAN LIVE **BRAVE**

YOU
CAN
LIVE
BRAVE

Finding Faith and Strength
When **Loving** an Addict Hurts

DENA L. WALL

MANYSEASONSPRESS
Mesa, Arizona • 2025

FIRST EDITION

You Can Live Brave: Finding Faith and Strength
When Loving an Addict Hurts

Copyright © 2025 Dena L. Wall

✱

MANY**SEASONS**PRESS

Published by Many Seasons Press
an Imprint of Multimedia Publishing Project
123 N. Centennial Way, Suite 105
Mesa, Arizona 85201
480-939-9689 | ManySeasonsPress.com

Book designed by Yolie Hernandez
(AZBookDesigner@icloud.com)

Paperback ISBN: 978-1-956203-74-5

◗⌒◗⌒◗⌒

To my husband Kevin and my children Sophia and Zach.

You have walked this most difficult road with me, encouraging me along the way and speaking truth into my life as a mother. I will forever be grateful for your patience throughout this journey and for always pointing me closer to Christ.

You've experienced heartache too, and yet you've shown great strength and perseverance.

I love you deeply.

• • ● • •

TABLE OF CONTENTS

ACKNOWLEDGMENTS

TO MY HUSBAND, THANK YOU FOR YOUR ENCOURAGEMENT IN writing this book, even though it is a raw, unfiltered story of our life.

To my children, Sophia and Zach, thank you for your honesty in expressing the pain of growing up with an older sister who wasn't always kind.

To my girlfriends, who call me weekly just to make sure I'm okay, always ready to listen. I understand how selfless that is—our lives are busy, yet you consistently make time for me. I will forever be grateful for your hope, encouragement, patience, understanding, and most of all, your prayers. I know how blessed I am to have such loving, level-headed friends. You are in my life forever.

To my mother—and to my father, who is now in heaven—thank you for answering my thousands of tearful phone calls, offering advice and lifting me in prayer. Thank you for spending quality time with our children over the years, giving me much-needed rest. I will always treasure the last conversation I had with my dad, which was about the very topic of this book. I can still hear his voice and wisdom in my head.

To my counselors, Steve and Lynne—what can I say? You've met me in moments of desperation, rearranged your schedules, and helped me stay grounded. I will always be thankful for your honest insights, for pointing me to Christ, and for helping me understand that addiction stems from the addict's choices—not from being a bad mother.

And most importantly, to God. I am forever grateful for the Bible, and for the wisdom and truth You have given us. Thank You for the privilege of prayer—at any time, in any place. I have felt Your presence many times. You alone have given me the strength and clarity that could only come from You.

If you don't really know God, take a moment now. Bow your head. Ask Him to forgive you and come into your life. Then find a church community and watch the Lord begin to move in your life— no matter what you are facing.

INTRODUCTION

TAKE A LOOK TO YOUR LEFT AND RIGHT AS YOU SIT IN CHURCH, and I guarantee there is someone in your row affected by the painful sting of addiction. As they sit in church with maybe some of their children, the memories of the missing child who's not there flood their minds—sometimes it's difficult to concentrate on the sermon. Last week, I noticed a mother walking down the aisle at church carrying a bag of crayons and a coloring book, with her five-year-old child holding her hand. And I wanted to blurt out, "Please. Take me back to that time again!" In the same breath, I also wanted to cry out, "God, why is our child still missing?"

Then the memories start to flood your mind, and you wonder how that little girl who loved coming to church could now be missing—out on the streets somewhere, where you can't save her. Some parents in this position go up for prayer, and some suffer in silence. But believe me, they are in every congregation and every neighborhood—wealthy or not. Maybe their child isn't missing like our daughter, but they are grieving beyond belief as they walk the confusing road of loving an addict.

This book was written for the parent navigating that painful path. My prayer is that it brings you hope, peace, suggestions on how to cope, and the assurance that you are not alone. Our journey is not over yet, so I pray that as you read our story, you'll know I completely understand your pain. And there is hope in the pain. You can get stronger and heal. Most of all, God sees your situation and wants to carry you through it all.

Blessings.

YOU CAN LIVE **BRAVE**

So do not fear, for I am with you;
do not be dismayed, for I am your God.
I will strengthen you and help you;
I will uphold you with my righteous right hand.
— Isaiah 41:10 (NIV)

• • • •

chapter one ❀

THE BLUEPRINT

IF I WERE SITTING IN A COFFEE SHOP WITH YOU RIGHT NOW, I'D WANT to give you a hug, because I know you are part of a group bound by broken dreams. Some broken dreams can be repaired and redirected, and some just lie on the floor in pieces. My hope is that these words will help you feel less alone—and realize that those pieces on the floor still have meaning. You can still pick yourself up and recreate a lovely, even joyful, life.

I'm sharing my personal journey here — a vulnerable thing to do — but I believe it's necessary to connect people—helping them understand that if others with broken dreams can continue living meaningful lives, maybe you can too. This book is short on purpose, since many readers don't have much free time. Each chapter offers helpful tips I've learned on my journey of navigating the world of loving someone with addiction.

At 59, I realized I had carried a plan for my entire life—confident that the winding paths would eventually lead to the blueprint I had sketched in my mind.

Did you have a blueprint for your life? Maybe you aimed to graduate at the top of your college class, only to discover that college didn't work out for you. Or maybe you expected to be married by a certain age with children—only to find yourself past childbearing age and still single. I've listened to hundreds of people over the years tell me how shocked or saddened they were because their lives didn't turn out the way they had planned.

Many people form detailed life blueprints at a young age, believing with certainty that life will simply follow the path they envisioned. I know I did.

There are different kinds of life blueprints. Some can still be achieved with effort, even when reality doesn't initially match. For instance, maybe you've always believed you would be financially secure. It's possible you grew up with financial security, so it never crossed your mind that this may not be how life would turn out for you. Maybe you have college degrees and solid work experience, but for whatever reason, your life is in financial distress. In this case, you could take a financial class to learn the steps towards financial freedom. You could consult someone you know who would take the time to look at your finances and help you get back on track. You could sell your large home and downsize or cut up your credit cards. You can make changes that help align your reality with your original life vision.

Then there's the other kind of blueprint—the one where there's absolutely nothing you can do to change it. If you're facing that version, as I am, then what are you going to do?

How do you keep going when the plan you held so tightly has veered off course? How do you cope with the pain of broken dreams and deep heartache? You're now facing a huge challenge that may bring confusion, sorrow, anxiety, and depression—just to name a few.

For me, that challenge is walking the unfamiliar path of a loved one suffering from addiction and holding onto hope for a missing child to come home.

I'm still in the middle of this crisis. I can relate to the grief, fear, anxiety, confusion, and deep sadness that can make your heart physically hurt. Even if your story doesn't involve addiction, I believe this book can help you face your own reality—one that didn't quite turn out the way you expected.

May these words encourage you to lift your head a little higher and perhaps take one small step toward something beautiful. Thank you for reading my personal story. May this book bring you peace—and help you live a beautiful life.

For it is God who works in you to will and to act in order to fulfill his good purpose.
— Philippians 2:13 (NIV)

• • • •

chapter two

MARRIAGE AND INFERTILITY

MY ENTIRE LIFE, I JUST KNEW MOTHERHOOD WAS IN THE PLAN. My favorite Christmas gift growing up was a baby doll given to me by my parents at the age of five. I remember rounding the corner of the living room and seeing "Baby Julie" sitting under the Christmas tree. She cried when you patted her back, and her eyelids opened and closed when you rocked her. Apparently, my mom stood in a long line waiting to purchase this baby doll for me.

Right from the start, I rocked this baby, pretended to feed her, took her on walks, and gently swaddled her before putting her to bed in a wooden cradle. I still have Baby Julie—and the cradle. I couldn't wait to be old enough to babysit the neighborhood children, and I would stuff my backpack with homemade cookies and games to bring to every job. Taking care of children just felt natural, fun, and easy for me. For some reason, I thought having and raising children would be easy too.

Growing up in a stable Christian home, my brother and I never caused problems for our parents, nor did any of my friends, so I can't recall ever being around children who created chaos or were involved in unhealthy situations. I participated in school activities, worked, did my homework, was involved in church, and had amazing friends. In short, I lived in a nice, warm, loving bubble—which I don't regret. Every dream I had for myself just seemed to come true. I landed great jobs, did well in college, dated kind people, and was surrounded by strong friendships.

So naturally, I created a blueprint for my life and imprinted it on my soul, believing life would unfold in that exact way with little upheaval. In hindsight, those were naive thoughts—but that's where I was.

Have you ever been jolted when your life plan suddenly takes a major turn? To say I was shocked by how far off course my blueprint ended up would be an understatement.

What do you do when you're left holding a heart that hurts so much you have to physically place your hand over it and remind yourself, you're not having a heart attack—it's a broken heart, cracked like the windowpane of your dreams.

Fast forward to age 28. I married a Christian man named Kevin, a physician who also came from a stable background. I remember how intelligent and even-tempered he was when we met. What really caught my attention was his leadership. He followed through on everything he said he would do (which can be rare in your twenties—just saying), and he seemed to make strong decisions with ease. Somehow, I just knew that quality would be important in my life.

He asked me to marry him after only six months of dating, but I had no doubt it was the right decision. My little life blueprint was moving along nicely. I worked for a stable company, holding a job that was fulfilling to me. At this time, my husband was enjoying all the aspects that come with building his practice. We built our first home in a quiet neighborhood, and we delighted in making it a home by planting flowers all along the front, wallpapering the kitchen, and shopping for furniture. We even purchased our first dog, Marlee, together. This home was filled with love, as we entertained quite a bit and loved having out-of-town guests stay there.

We decided to wait a few years before having children, and after four years of marriage, we were ready and excited to start our family. Children had always gravitated toward me, and I was thrilled at the idea of parenting—walks in the park, visiting the zoo, doing crafts, teaching them about Jesus, snuggling up for bedtime stories, and creating lifelong memories. We were so excited for that next chapter. Due to my upbringing, along with my husband's, it never occurred to me that parenting would be challenging. Yes, I understood kids would be kids and there might be some redirecting and time-outs. However, I truly believed I could effectively handle any small bumps in the road.

After a year of trying to conceive, my life began to show signs that it no longer matched the blueprint I was certain would unfold. After many months of not getting pregnant, we began the exhausting journey of tests—and more tests. Each passing month brought tears and the first real questions I had ever asked God.

I tried to hold onto my belief that God had a plan, but discouragement—and even anger—began to rise within me. I remember crying out of the blue at the grocery store, and I even snapped at a stranger once. The pain was building inside me. People constantly asked, "So when are you going to have kids?" (Please don't ask that question to anyone, by the way.)

Maybe it was just the obsessive state I was in, but it felt like every commercial was about baby products and everyone around me was getting pregnant. If I heard about one more teenager "accidentally" getting pregnant, I thought I might commit a felony. Not really—but you get what I'm saying.

We moved into a large, beautiful Victorian home with a wraparound porch on a gorgeous street, and several neighbors dropped by to introduce themselves—each asking, "So, do you have a bunch of children to fill up that house?" I remember stumbling over my words: "Oh... one day, for sure."

Little by little, that year, I felt myself shutting down. Most of my close friends were busy raising children, meeting up for playdates and time together. I mean, the kids needed bonding time, and the mothers needed a break as well. Although it was not intentional, I felt left out of the group. Most of those friends stayed home with their children, and I was still working. Deep down inside, I really wanted to begin a family and stay home with my children too. I would go to work and then just come home, with little effort to be social. I didn't want to talk about children at all. Dramatic? Yes—but it was all due to pain. I didn't want to talk to anyone. Loneliness filled the walls of our home—and my heart. Then we pursued more infertility testing and began trying different methods. A friend of mine had a connection to one of the top infertility specialists in the U.S., and he agreed to meet with us. We were so grateful for his wisdom and time.

We flew to Texas to review our test results. I still remember that day—sitting across his large maple desk. He was tall, with thick dark hair and an Italian accent. He exuded kindness, which I greatly appreciated given the intensity of the moment.

He had a folder on his desk with our results. Looking into our eyes with compassion, he told us we would not be able to conceive naturally. My eyes instantly filled with tears. I wanted to run out of that office to some faraway place where I didn't have to face the trauma. Would it be strange if I just ran through the streets of San Antonio and didn't stop? Probably. But that's exactly what I wanted to do.

We left the meeting in silence and boarded a plane that same day back to Arizona. I stared out the window, not saying a word, trying to hold back the tears while my mind raced with questions: How did this happen to us? We honored God in our relationship. I followed the Lord my entire life. We had the means to offer a stable home to a child. I had spent a year begging God to let me be a mother.

Now what?

hindsight helping tips

• • • • •

- Take a timeout. If you're facing something difficult as a couple, don't push each other away. Give yourselves time to be still. Life-altering situations need space, not pressure.

- Allow your spouse or friend to grieve in their own way. If they need silence, allow it. If they need to talk, make space for that too. Men and women often grieve differently—extend grace.

- Remember that life isn't over when change shows up. God always has a plan.

- Life-altering experiences can lead to a deeper relationship with God, who holds all the answers. Now is the time to ask Him what He has planned for you.

- Meditate on Philippians 2:13: "For it is God who works in you to will and to act in order to fulfill his good purpose." There's always purpose in the pain.

- Place your hand over your heart and tell yourself... You're going to be alright.

NOTES: _____

_____

_____

_____

_____

The Lord is close to the brokenhearted
and saves those who are crushed in spirit.
— Psalm 34:18 (NIV)

chapter three 🌸

ADOPTION

WE TOOK SOME TIME TO PRAY ABOUT OUR NEXT STEPS toward becoming parents. As a couple, we made the decision not to disclose what our test results revealed, as this was a very personal journey. We began asking ourselves the hard questions: Do we follow the medical route? Do we pursue adoption? Or do we choose not to have children?

I always had a heart for adoption—ever since I worked in a Romanian orphanage one summer before I was married. My husband wasn't opposed to adoption, but we didn't want to rush into anything while the wounds were still fresh. One thing we both knew: we always wanted children and had pictured them in our lives. We believed God would not have given us such a strong desire if He didn't want us to have children.

Once we decided to pursue adoption, we began the emotional process of getting certified and meeting young birth mothers. Every step in the process brought hope—but also felt like a knife to the heart. The mounds of paperwork, the letters our family members had to write about us, and having a professional inspect our home—it was painful. All these people having natural births didn't need to be inspected or approved to have a baby. Why did we have to prove ourselves? So many procedures—just to determine if we were "good enough" to adopt a child.

Many nights I spent on my knees, crying out to God, asking why these young, unmarried girls were given the gift of having a baby without having to go through this approval process. I became angry with God and withdrew. I never left my faith, but there were seasons where I grew bitter and quiet with Him. I used to sit in an antique rocking chair in our large Victorian home, day after day, staring out the window with my face wet with tears. I don't mean to be dramatic—but the pain was deep and dark. Some of you know exactly what I'm talking about.

At this point, I just couldn't bear going to baby showers or anything to do with children. I lost friends over this—they thought I was being selfish. I was genuinely happy for these families, but the pain was too much for me at the time. We lived in a small development of 36 homes arranged in a big circle. I would walk that circle over and over, praying that one day my dream of becoming a mother would come true. I'm not sure how many pairs of tennis shoes I went through, but it was quite a few. Even during the moments I was stomping my feet at God, telling Him this wasn't my blueprint, I still believed there had to be a plan.

One year later, we received a call from the adoption agency: a young, unmarried girl had looked at our profile letter and wanted to meet us. We'd already had several unsuccessful meetings with birth mothers. Either they chose another couple, or they decided to keep the baby. Each time brought excitement—and nerves. What questions do we ask? What will they ask us? Think of the nerves you'd have before your dream job interview—then multiply that by fifty.

We walked into the agency's meeting room, where the birth mother and her mother were waiting. The conversation was easy. The birth mother seemed kind. Her sister had experienced an unplanned pregnancy, and their mother didn't want another daughter to go through the hardship of raising a child at a young age. The birth father was in jail.

After a few weeks of meetings, we all agreed it felt like a good fit. My husband and I were thrilled to finally become parents. I attended several of the birth mother's doctor appointments and prayed for a healthy baby in every way. When I learned the baby was a girl, I was overjoyed. We had already chosen a beautiful name, and I began walking around the house saying it out loud.

The birth mother even allowed me to be present for the birth—a gesture I found incredibly thoughtful. I was also given the opportunity to cut the cord. Witnessing a birth is a miracle; I was overcome with emotion and could barely see through my tears. At the same time, it was a bit awkward—I was the only person in the room not directly related to the birth mother. I tried to show compassion for what she was going through, while also feeling the joy of holding this beautiful baby. It's hard to be in the middle of that emotional contrast.

Thankfully, the hospital staff was understanding and kind. I've heard that's not always the case during adoptions. Because it was against hospital policy to transfer the baby directly to the adoptive parents, we all walked out to the parking lot together. It felt cold and strange. The birth mother kissed the baby and placed her in the car seat. We hugged her and her family, then put the baby in the car and drove away. I looked at my husband and said, "It feels like we just stole a baby."

We felt immense love for this child instantly—even before she was born—and deep compassion for the birth family. Once home, we took turns holding her while friends and family rushed over to meet this precious little girl. A friend even had one of those large stork cutouts placed in the front yard to announce her arrival.

However, my dreams of showering love on a child, creating a stable home, teaching her spiritual truths, and building a creative life together did not fully come to pass.

I want to pause here and say—we did have many wonderful experiences together. She was a gregarious, funny, adorable little girl. She loved people. At a party once, with fifty people in our home, she exclaimed, "Is anyone else coming?" She was always on the go, ready to explore life. We even had to have a police officer talk to her when she was five about "stranger danger" because she would walk up and talk to anyone. She connected us to so many people with her outgoing nature—and she truly was a cute little girl.

I also want to make clear: this is not meant to discourage adoption in any way. This chapter is about finding encouragement when life takes an unexpected turn. We later adopted two additional children—a biological brother and sister—whose birth parents struggled with addiction. They have walked straight and wonderful paths in life. Both continue to be a blessing to our family, and I was able to love and nurture them in all the ways I had dreamed of. They too have had to endure the impact of their sister's choices, which I'll discuss in a later chapter.

From the beginning, our oldest daughter's life was marked by hurt, disappointment, and trauma. Yes, there were good times—when she decided to behave. When she was doing what she wanted to do, she was lovely. I could always bring her to a party, and she'd charm the other children. Her vocabulary was advanced, and her energy never-ending. When going somewhere she enjoyed, she was engaging and sweet.

Once, when she was about three, she sat in the front of a grocery cart and spotted an elderly man in a cowboy hat. She leaned over and said, "How are you doing, little cowboy?" He smiled and replied, "Doing great, Little Princess." Every outing was about people for her. She even loved going to the dentist—at five years old, holding her deer stuffed animal, she tapped the dentist's arm during the exam. Afterward, she jumped down from the chair and said, "I love you, doctor." She had her super adorable moments.

However, from age two to now (she is 27), it has been a daily rollercoaster. You may think I'm exaggerating when I say *every single day*—but unless you've lived through something like this, it's hard to understand. I could fill a book three inches thick with the stories.

For example: While outgoing, she never made close friends—largely due to her compulsive lying, which began in third grade. One day, I left two donuts on the counter and told her we'd eat them later. A few hours later, they were gone. I gave her a chance to admit it, saying I hadn't eaten them—and she denied everything.

Another time, a police officer knocked on the door. Someone had called 911 from our home. I was upstairs with our two younger children doing schoolwork. Our daughter, then in fourth grade, was downstairs where there was a phone. When I asked if she had called, she flat-out denied it. I gave her another chance and said, "Well, it wasn't us upstairs. Was it the dog?" She looked the officer in the eye and said it was the dog.

There were calls from the horse barn where she took lessons, saying she wasn't caring for the horses. Parents in the neighborhood contacted me about her misbehavior. Still, we loved her. I threw myself into finding solutions—counseling, research, support groups—while also running a household, supporting my marriage, and helping our other children with their own challenges. Many nights, I cried silently into my pillow.

Outwardly, it may have looked like we had it all: beautiful home, Christian school, successful husband, sweet little family. But inwardly, I was dying a slow death of loneliness. Maybe you've felt that too.

School was a nightmare. She avoided doing her work and told conflicting stories. "I forgot it at school." I'd call the school janitor to open her locker - nothing was ever there. Then she'd tell the teacher it was home, and this scenario continued for years. She'd ask to use the school bathroom and stay gone most of the class. She was polite and friendly to staff and classmates, but she refused direction from authority.

I'm a type A personality. I couldn't imagine *not* doing homework—so I hovered. Yes, I became a helicopter parent. I now understand the importance of letting them fail, but back then, I was fixated on fixing everything.

Our daughter was clever, funny, and a born leader. At age 5, when no one stopped at her lemonade stand, she said, "Well, looks like I'm going door to door." But there was always another side.

She stole our credit card multiple times, lied about where she was, was secretly mean to her siblings (which I only recently found out), and took friends to our country club and charged things to our account.

As a teenager, we caught her chatting on the phone with a stranger in Florida, who was trying to convince her to visit him. She never met this man, and he was constantly texting her to come to Florida. I started shaking and sweating as complete terror ran through my body. A man was trying to get my daughter to the bus depot to get to Florida? It was a nightmare. My husband grabbed her phone and let's just say the conversation wasn't pretty. I've never seen him so angry. So we were always on high alert trying to see what she might be planning next and how to stop it.

Eventually, we sent her to a Christian boarding school out of state at age 16. After 40 years, the staff told us they had never seen anything like it. She refused to do any work—even though it meant solitary confinement. I was embarrassed running into other moms in our town from school who asked where she was. I didn't know anyone else who had sent their child away. But we were desperate, and our home greatly needed peace.

At this point, I have to fast-forward to when our daughter turned 18. Stay with me. Understanding the pain is important—because it may resonate with your own.

~hindsight helping tips~

• • • •

- Stay the course and get your child into consistent counseling. We were inconsistent because it was frustrating and our other kids needed attention, but consistency matters.

- Get support—for yourself and with your spouse.

- Have your child tested. She was diagnosed with ADHD, but I now believe more was going on. Trust your gut if you think one diagnosis doesn't explain everything.

- Let them fail. I didn't see it then, but failure can be a gift.

- Take parenting breaks. Call a trusted friend to help.

- Don't let one child dominate the home. Spend intentional time with your other children, too.

- This is not your fault. Don't beat yourself up over a wayward child. Even Jesus had wayward children—just look at Adam and Eve.

NOTES: _____

_____

_____

_____

_____

_____

I am the vine; you are the branches. If you remain in me and I in you, you will bear much fruit; apart from me you can do nothing.
— John 15:5 (NIV)

chapter four 🌸

HOLDING ON FOR DEAR LIFE

OUR DAUGHTER FINALLY GRADUATED HIGH SCHOOL, BUT THERE was no celebration at all. It had been a constant battle—fighting her tooth and nail to get homework done all four years. Graduation party invitations were flooding our mailbox, and I wanted to throw a party for our firstborn too. But there wasn't much to celebrate. She hadn't accomplished much at the boarding school, so we brought her back home. During her final semester, she was enrolled in an online program.

It was me, my husband, and our daughter sitting at the kitchen table every day with our laptops, trying to help her finish her last few classes. Honestly, I think I wanted it more than she did. In my mind, I thought, *Let's just get her through school and on to a full-time job.* Maybe that would be the answer to this madness. My husband and I were exhausted as we were managing our business and taking care of two additional children.

At this point, we laid down the blueprint we'd carried for our children to attend college, because she had no interest. I let go of that dream and began researching trade schools. I drove her to equestrian programs since she loved horses—maybe she could gain the skills to work with them. She didn't want to do the work. I arranged meetings with technical schools because she was talented in culinary arts and photography. She said no to both.

Thanks to her gregarious personality, she landed a job at a pet resort. We were excited—it seemed like a perfect fit, especially since she loved animals. But soon, she started lying about her work schedule, hanging out with questionable people, and not responding to calls late at night.

The stress and strain were affecting everyone in the family. My husband and I argued constantly about how to handle her. One minute I wanted to enforce strict consequences, while Kevin wanted to take a softer approach. Then I'd try compassion, and he'd want to lay down firmer rules. We truly tried to be on the same page, but the constant behavioral issues made it hard to know what to do in each situation.

We spent countless hours in counseling. Kevin and I often attended sessions together, but I sat through more of them alone—crying, blaming myself as a mother. I'd lie awake night after night, staring at the ceiling, wondering where she was and what we were going to do.

Our other two children—super compliant by nature—would retreat to their rooms, wondering when the next episode with their sister would unfold. It was stressful for them too, and at times they felt abandoned. We were constantly out looking for her or answering disturbing calls about what kind of trouble she was in.

One night, the four of us were eating dinner when we got a call that our daughter had been bucked off a horse and was lying unconscious in a field. We had to leave our other children at the table and rush out. Kevin ran into the field. She eventually woke up but refused to come home or go to the hospital. He kept pleading, "Just get in the car. Please, just get in the car." She refused. We left—our hearts racing and breaking.

Try coming home after that and acting normal for your other kids. It's nearly impossible.

hindsight helping tips

• • • •

- Take care of yourself. High stress can become a health issue. Dive into projects you love. For me, exercise is crucial, nutrition is key, and reading the Bible brings peace.

- Pray. Pray. Pray. Sit in your child's room when they aren't home and pray over it.

- Get psychological testing for your child. We did this, but the doctors didn't truly understand our daughter. We should have gotten a second opinion. If your gut tells you the diagnosis is off—get another one.

- John 15:5 — "I am the vine; you are the branches. If you remain in me and I in you, you will bear much fruit; apart from me you can do nothing." We are not in control. Lay the burden before the Lord. Tell Him to take over—and go about your day in peace.

NOTES: _____

_____

_____

_____

_____

_____

_____

You will keep in perfect peace
those whose minds are steadfast,
because they trust in you.
— Isaiah 26:3 (NIV)

chapter five ✿

THINGS STARTED TO RAMP UP

AT 18 YEARS OLD, OUR OLDEST DAUGHTER WALKED OUT OF THE house and told us she was moving in with a random person she had met while working a few weeks at a fast-food restaurant near our home. She would pop in and out of our lives unannounced, manipulating the person she was staying with to let her live there— even though she barely worked and eventually lost the job. Yet the girl still let her stay.

One time, our daughter came home covered in bedbug bites, trying to pass them off as an allergy. But my husband is a physician and knew it wasn't an allergic reaction. We, of course, tried talking to her—urging her to leave the filthy place she was living, come home, and start again. But she had met a man in the complex who happened to be a fentanyl dealer. We haven't seen her in six years.

We might hear from her every couple of years, for about 15 minutes. Each time is bittersweet—because she's always high. The calls are deeply stressful, not just emotionally, but mentally. They come at completely random times. Once, she called during a funeral, and I had to excuse myself to take it. I never know when the next call might come, so I answer every random number that comes to my phone.

That time, she told me she was in jail. *My daughter was in jail?* I've spent my whole life as president of the "follow the rules" club, so to hear those words sent me into a tailspin. How could this happen to our family? I have enormous respect for law enforcement—I rush to log into traffic school the moment I get a citation. Yet here I was— leaning into the fact that I had a daughter in jail.

I remember hanging my head as I tried to keep her on the line, stunned that we were having this conversation. When she said she had to hang up but would call me in the morning, I believed her. The next morning, I waited. Then I called the jail, only to be told, "We let her go."

Let her go? Without notifying her mother? That's the system. She wasn't considered a major threat. Everything in me wanted to scream, *But that's my daughter! You let her go, and now I don't know when I'll hear from her again.*

She didn't have a phone. She had one when she lived at home, but after failing to follow rules, we canceled it. We tried providing a prepaid flip phone, but it was stolen the same week. I'd receive random calls from strangers saying she was being abused or was in danger. They gave me cross streets and descriptions of vehicles. I'd call the police, but they could never find her. This happened more than once.

The calls always came to my cell phone—never when my husband was around. I don't know why, but that's how it happened. Those calls rattled me to my core. I'd pace the floor all night, praying, heart pounding, and crying so hard my eyes would be swollen shut. Then I'd get up the next day to manage our business and oversee our kids' schoolwork, pretending everything was normal while my world was falling apart.

Eventually, I started experiencing vertigo regularly. I became convinced hereditary heart problems were catching up to me. My sleep patterns were a mess. I was falling apart physically and emotionally.

When she did call, the conversations were just as hard. We'd beg to come get her—but she was never in the same place and always said she wasn't ready. You never really understand what someone's "rock bottom" is. To me, living in a constant state of fear and survival on the streets would be rock bottom. She grew up in a gated community, surrounded by love and faith. But again, the words echo in my heart: *I don't know, but God knows.*

Once, a friend's husband said, "I'd hire the best detective to find her." We did. To no avail. It's incredibly hard to find someone who doesn't want to be found. We filed missing persons reports in different cities. But once they're over 18, the report is closed if they're found—and the authorities don't have to notify the family.

What's the point of that? I can't call every jail in the country. Sometimes she'll tell me where she is, and I'll want to jump in the car and drive the streets looking for her—but it's not safe, and I never know if she's telling the truth. No phone. No address. No trusted friends to call.

So you wait.

Maybe you're waiting too—for a child to come home, a loved one to find recovery, a marriage to heal, or a financial burden to lift. What do you do when your blueprint no longer matches your reality?

The mind is powerful. It will take you to dark places. You start to believe it's your fault—that you messed up somewhere, that you are to blame. I've had thoughts of ending my life, convinced that my poor mothering must have pushed her away. Thank God I verbalized those thoughts to trusted friends and family. I've never been prone to thinking like that, and I now know those thoughts aren't true.

If you're dealing with a prodigal, you constantly wonder: *Are they okay? Are they alive?*

This kind of waiting doesn't have a timeline. When you're expecting a baby, you know it's about nine months. When waiting for a job interview result, there's a typical time frame. But this kind of waiting? It's waking up every day wondering, *"Is this the day the nightmare ends?"* And going to sleep knowing you'll have to be strong again tomorrow.

And yet—it's during the waiting that you decide: Will this break me or make me stronger? These moments build grit, discipline, determination, and perseverance that ripple through every area of your life—and can impact others for the better.

You know the situation isn't good, so your mind begins to imagine all kinds of danger. You cry out to God, "When will the pain stop?"

Recently, I ran into a friend I hadn't seen in years. Our daughters went to the same small Christian school and used to swim and play together. I didn't want to ask about her daughter, because that would lead to her asking about mine. But she eagerly shared anyway: her daughter just received her master's degree and is expecting a baby.

Master's degree? Last time I spoke to my daughter, she was talking about maybe getting a tent and living in California.

I smiled for my friend. I was genuinely happy for her. But how can you not walk away from a conversation like that feeling heavy? My daughter is missing—on drugs, with no trace of her life.

Many times, I've clenched my fists at God, angry that my life's blueprint doesn't match my reality. A counselor once told me: *You don't know real prayer until your eyelashes hit the carpet fibers.* I believe that. I know that.

And then I think of Mary, the mother of Jesus. She probably didn't plan to be pregnant before marriage—certainly not with the Son of God. She had to tell Joseph and hope he believed her. Her life didn't follow the "blueprint"—but her obedience changed the world.

Was it Jonah's plan to live in a whale's belly? Yet through that trial, he brought a city to repentance. Moses was adopted into royalty and likely didn't expect to flee for his life or kill a man. But God used him to lead a nation to freedom.

These men and women of the Bible were used to change the world—but I doubt their plans looked anything like what God had in store.

When I share my story, people often ask: "How do you get up every day and go about your life while living in a nightmare?"

If you have heartache—whether it looks like mine or something else—what do you do with it?

I can tell you this: my heart has physically ached. I even saw a cardiologist, because I began having breathing issues and pain in my heart. Test after test came back normal. I wanted to tell the doctor about the 2:00 a.m. phone calls, the strange messages from strangers, the desperate prayers in the middle of the night.

This is heartache at the highest level. And it takes a toll.

Some people mask their pain by becoming addicts—whether through shopping, food, constant busyness, drinking, or anxiety. But anxiety is often a sign that we're trying to stay in control, and God wants us to release that control to Him.

God parted the Red Sea (Exodus 14:21–29), created the heavens and the earth (Genesis 1:1–31), and made human beings in His image (Genesis 1:27). What makes us think we're meant to carry anything in this life alone?

If we don't grieve in healthy ways, our pain spills out—usually in harmful ways.

When did I start believing I had to fix everything? Many moms fall into that trap. We're managers of the household, and if you combine that with a driven personality - it's a perfect storm. And we want answers now.

Nowhere in the Bible do we see God in a hurry. So why do we expect Him to answer us quickly?

hindsight helping tips

• • • •

- Reading the Bible. This is the most important thing I do. The Psalms are my refuge—David cries out to God, too. I discipline myself to read daily and lean into the truth that God loves me and is in control. If we fully understood God's love, it would heal so much.

- Prayer. I can't even count how many times I pray each day— while driving, cooking, walking, showering, drying my hair. I pray for God to give our daughter strength and clarity, and to remind her she is His child.

- Gift giving. I mail little gifts to people regularly. On my daughter's birthday, I ask God who needs a surprise gift—and send one in her honor. It helps me cope.

- Exercise. This is critical for me. It keeps me focused and lifts my mood. I've added Pilates and pickleball to my routine, and I'm meeting new people, which I love. Just move—find a walking buddy and start.

- Reading. I read about four books a month now—some on healing, but I also love biographies and business books. Reading shifts my mind from fixating on my daughter.

- Serving. Whether it's helping someone organize, run errands, or drop off food, serving others brings healing.

- Crafting. I have a craft studio with a door I can shut! It's my happy place—filled with ribbons, glue, and paper. I make cards and fun gifts and feel peaceful in that space.

- Lean into your pain. Years ago, I ran into a mom from our daughter's elementary school. I dreaded the question, "How are your kids?" question. I almost lied—but I told the truth. It was hard, but freeing. Now, I can tell our story without crying every time. I'm not skipping away in joy, but I leave it with the Lord.

- Turn off the noise. I don't watch TV much, but even so—turn it off. Turn off the radio. Walk slowly. Eat slowly. Drive calmly. Sit in a chair for 20 minutes with your eyes closed and ask God to speak. You'll be amazed what that silence can do for your body and mind.

NOTES: _____

_____

_____

_____

_____

_____

_____

_____

_____

_____

...for whenever our heart condemns us, God is
greater than our heart, and he knows everything.
— 1 John 3:20 (ESV)

~chapter six~ ❀

THE "I DON'T KNOW" THEORY

THIS LITTLE *"I DON'T KNOW"* METHOD IS SOMETHING I DEVELOPED —and it has brought my heart great peace. When you're in a life-altering situation, most of the time you really can't figure out exactly what happened that got you to this point. You can't get into the minds of others and fully understand their behaviors. And if mental illness is involved, it's even more difficult. You just don't know what led that person to where they are now.

I've beaten myself up believing the lie that our daughter is in this situation because of something I did. That I wasn't a good enough mother. That I didn't recognize the signs early enough. That I should've put her in a different school. That I should've looked more closely at her birth parents' background. That I should've switched counselors.

Maybe these are thoughts you've had in your own situation. *She's gone because I yelled at her that one time. If I'd been a better Christian, God wouldn't have punished me like this.*

The mind plays serious tricks on you.

What I've learned—through many hours of reading and counseling—is that sometimes, you just don't know what happened. And you may never know the root cause. Once, our pastor asked me, "Our family just finished painting our word for the year on wooden boards this weekend. So, Dena, what's your word for the year?"

I replied, "Well, I have three: I. Don't. Know."

He said, "That's not really spiritual."

I told him, "I'm not trying to be super spiritual. These words bring me peace."

Sometimes we may never fully understand why our life blueprint doesn't match our reality. When those haunting thoughts creep in, I simply say, *I don't know—but God knows.* That's the key. I am human. He is God. He is allowing this path for a reason, so I will trust Him as I always have.

Maybe you did something that altered the course of your life. Maybe it really was your fault. Well, there's grace in that too. God's love for you never changes. And He can redirect your life at any time—if you're willing to let Him.

So let Him.

hindsight helping tips

. . . . .

- The next time you ask yourself questions like, *"What happened? Did I do something to cause this person to use drugs? Were they so unhappy with our family that they just left?"*—tell yourself: I don't know, but God knows. Then move on with your day.

- If needed, ask for forgiveness for anything you may have done—but know this: most of the material I've read, along with advice from counselors, says it's the addict's choice.

- 1 John 3:20 – "For whenever our heart condemns us, God is greater than our heart, and He knows everything." We are not equipped to fully understand mental illness, addiction, or anxiety—and neither are you.

- A counselor once told me something every parent should remember: You shouldn't take full credit for the kids who turn out great—or full blame for the ones who take a wrong turn. It's not about you. People make their own choices. Some children are simply born more compliant and drawn to doing the right thing.

NOTES: _____

_____

_____

_____

_____

- Be very mindful of your self-talk. It directly affects your energy and your decision-making. You're in training. And training is hard—it pushes you in ways that may not feel natural. It's more natural to think negatively. But trusting and staying hopeful? That takes effort.

- Build good habits. Do Navy SEALs have disciplined habits? Of course—they push their minds and bodies beyond limits. Do high-level athletes rely on discipline? Yes—that's what makes them great. You can too.

- You don't have to fix the situation. Let that truth sink in until you believe it—and rest in it. God has answers and paths for you that you could never come up with on your own.

NOTES: _____

_____

_____

_____

_____

_____

_____

_____

_____

"Sometimes we may never fully understand why our life blueprint doesn't match our reality. When those haunting thoughts creep in, I simply say, *I don't know— but God knows.* That's the key. I am human. He is God. He is allowing this path for a reason, so I will trust Him as I always have."

I will instruct you and teach you in the way you should go;
I will counsel you with my loving eye on you.
— Psalm 32:8 (NIV)

chapter seven

NOT AT THE END

I CAN'T TELL YOU HOW MANY TIMES I'VE HEARD A SERMON OR A speaker share a story that wraps up with a happy ending—how God worked everything out in the end. Or how many movies (even Christian ones) offer the same kind of resolution.

All the while, I'm sitting there asking myself an important question: "What happens when it doesn't end well?"

How does a person move through life with meaning, purpose, and enthusiasm when the ending they expected never comes? And is it even possible to have a life filled with goodness while navigating heartbreak?

Maybe you're just in the beginning stages of a devastating situation—a sudden divorce, a job demotion, the loss of a child. Even a major move across the country can wreak havoc on a person or family. Or maybe, like me, you've been walking a painful road for years—caring for a chronically ill loved one or dealing with a child's addiction.

When drugs entered our daughter's life, the stress and strain amplified. But the truth is, we've been walking through pain with her for her entire life. There were times I didn't think I was going to make it. Like, seriously—I didn't think I could get through another day.

It shocked me, because I had always seen myself as a strong person. But I didn't know how to navigate this mountain, and no one around me was going through anything like it.

That's where the loneliness hit hard. It felt like I was backpacking a giant mountain—with no trail, no map, and no guide—and my backpack was weighing down my entire body.

At least my husband had work to escape to. I was at home with three children, trying to manage normal parenting while juggling teacher meetings, parent meetings, and counseling sessions—all sparked by one child's disruptive behavior.

I was called to 7 a.m. meetings with my daughter's teachers—multiple times—as we all tried to work together to help her. I felt terrible that these hardworking educators had to come in early to meet with me. I'd sit at the table and cry as they asked questions, hoping I could give them insight.

But the truth is, I still don't have the answers.

I have a few ideas, but I'm not confident about the root cause of her behaviors. Maybe I'll never know the answers to my burning questions:

- Was this all just attention-seeking?

- Were there more drugs in her system at birth than I was told?

- Did some kind of trauma happen in her early years that I never discovered?

These questions send me spinning—like I'm on a hamster wheel, going round and round.

That's where the "I Don't Know" concept helps. I say those words—along with *"But God knows"*—and I keep going.

~hindsight helping tips~

• • • • •

- Tell yourself, "Get off the hamster wheel," and go complete a task. Sometimes you'll never get the answers you're looking for. For me, it helps to do something productive—bake, cook, clean, write a note to someone. One night I was so stressed, I painted the entire garage. That's extreme—but you get the idea.

- If you're a parent of a young child and attending endless meetings, consider switching schools. Looking back, I was trying to force our daughter into a mold that didn't fit. The private school simply wasn't a good match for her. Would the problems have followed her elsewhere? Possibly. But now I understand that the learning style just wasn't right for her.

- Find good friends. This circle might be small. Some people just don't have the depth of compassion needed to walk through hard things. But you need friends who will speak truth to you and walk beside you. If you don't have those people yet, I recommend joining a church group or an Al-Anon group for support.

- Remind yourself: even if your desired outcome hasn't happened, you can still live a beautiful, meaningful life. Years ago, I couldn't imagine believing that. But it's true. I'm now moving forward—participating in things I enjoy and serving others through my God-given gifts.

NOTES: _____

_____

"For I know the plans I have for you," declares the Lord, "plans to prosper you and not to harm you, plans to give you hope and a future.
— Jeremiah 29:11 (NIV)

chapter eight

THE CIRCLE METHOD

HERE'S ANOTHER CONCEPT I FORMULATED THAT HAS GREATLY helped me walk this difficult path. I call it *"The Circle."* I drew it out years ago—stick figures and all, due to my lack of artistic skills. I drew myself, my husband, my children, friends, and my parents—all inside a little bubble.

Then I drew another circle: everyone else stayed in the bubble, but I was outside of it. I hope you can picture this with me.

That's when a lightbulb went off in my head. Apart from all these meaningful roles—being a wife, mother, friend, sister, and daughter—I am a child of God. And with that identity comes both responsibility and peace.

He's got me. He's got you.

Outside of all those responsibilities, God has a specific plan for me in this world—and He has one for you, too. He gave each of us unique gifts and talents to bring light into the world. And Lord knows—we need more light.

So yes, our daughter is still missing, and yes, there is pain every single day. But I believe there is still a purpose for my life here on earth. And for yours too.

What does that look like in real time? At this point, I know what my gifts are—and what they are not. I'm definitely not the person to handle anything involving numbers (I blame that on my third-grade math teacher—just kidding). But if you put me in a creative space or ask me to think outside the box, I come alive.

One way I use my gifts is by coming up with creative ways to appreciate our company's staff. I love encouraging others through meaningful gift-giving. I mean, who doesn't love getting a fun package in the mail? (I know I do.)

Organizing appreciation dinners is another outlet for me. Every year, I decorate the house and set a festive Valentine's table—sprinkled with red and pink hearts. Lasagna (red!) is usually on the menu, along with small token gifts at each place setting and plenty of chocolate treats. You don't need a romantic partner to celebrate love. You can still celebrate—even if someone is missing from the table.

What I do know is that God's plan for my life does not involve living in constant anxiety.

Does anxiety still knock on the door of my heart? Absolutely. But I fight to keep it from settling in. God's plan does not involve me staying in bed all day, afraid to face life. It doesn't have me crying myself to sleep every night anymore. Sure, some days bring more tears than others, but I refuse to live in constant misery—for the sake of my friends, my family, and myself.

I know God has more for me. And for you. Even as we navigate this confusing, winding road.

If you are a parent walking through addiction, and all the heartbreak and disruption that comes with it—you can still reclaim your life. You don't have to allow the addicted person in your life to control your life. They have choices. And so do you.

You can be there when they're ready. You can tell them you love them when you get the chance to hear their voice. But you can also choose to live a beautiful, meaningful life now.

You can get your energy back. You can do the hard work to grow stronger. Maybe that means committing to read the Bible daily and letting God encourage you with truth. Maybe it's time to chase that dream you've always carried—even if chaos still surrounds you.

You can call that school and finally pursue the degree. You can reach out to that nonprofit and start volunteering. You can take the cooking class. Sign up for the art workshop. You can move forward.

I've wasted so many hours being paralyzed by pain because of my daughter's decisions. I once planned a beautiful 50th birthday party—lunch at a gorgeous Scottsdale resort with spa treatments for all my closest friends. My husband was covering the cost.

Then, the week before, our daughter started acting out in major ways—calling me in the middle of the night high, showing up unannounced with strangers. I cancelled the party.

I regret that now. I had the chance to be with the people I love, and instead I spent days unable to get out of bed.

I also spent many hours crying on my father's shoulder about this situation—never knowing he would pass away suddenly. That time with him was precious, and I now wish I had spent more of it being present with him instead of being consumed by pain.

But today—joy and peace have returned. I've come to understand I can still pursue my dreams and find joy—even while my daughter is missing.

I want my experience to help you wake up to the life you *do* have right now. It takes work. And I've realized: no one else can do that work for me—or for you.

We have to make the changes. We have to give ourselves grace.

Every day won't be perfect. But it's our responsibility to show up for the life we've been given.

Not perfectly—just faithfully.

~hindsight helping tips~

.....

- Take a piece of paper and write down 10 things you love to do. Many of these will be things you loved as a child but pushed aside in adulthood.

- Pick one thing from your list and take action. Sign up for a class. Join a gym. Walk in the park once a week and gradually build up from there.

- If other areas of your life are adding stress, consider taking practical steps. Is your home unaffordable? Call a realtor. Is your job draining you? Reach out to a recruiter or start looking online. Taking just *one step* toward something positive can boost your energy and clear your mind.

- Remember: you matter. You are important to the people around you. They need you to become the best version of yourself—not the most perfect version—just the one who shows up with hope.

NOTES: _____

_____

_____

_____

_____

_____

"But today—
joy and peace
have returned.
I've come to
understand I can
still pursue my
dreams and find
joy—even while
my daughter
is missing."

Trust in the Lord with all your heart
and lean not on your own understanding;
in all your ways submit to him,
and he will make your paths straight..
— Proverbs 3:5-6 (NIV)

chapter nine

WHAT DOES MY TRUST LOOK LIKE?

EVEN THOUGH I'VE BEEN A COMMITTED CHRISTIAN SINCE THE AGE of seven—following and serving the Lord in various ways throughout my life—I realized I struggled with something: complete trust in God.

I'm not really sure why trust has been such an issue for me. From what I've read, many women who struggle with trust do so because of a poor relationship with their father. But I had a wonderful relationship with my earthly father. I could trust him to always be available, to tell me the truth, to protect me.

I also have close friends I trust with my deepest secrets—friends I know would take those secrets to their grave. So why do I still find trust difficult?

I think, for me, it's because having a child now addicted to drugs and missing is so far beyond my understanding. It's too big for me to comprehend. Maybe that's you, too. One day, they're your little girl—and then one day, they're simply gone.

Do I truly trust that God has me in the palm of His hand—even when the road ahead is so foggy I can only see one step at a time?

For years, trust wasn't really a challenge for me. Life had a steady rhythm. But when a bulldozer of a situation crashes into your world, can you honestly say, *"Yes, God still has a plan"*?

These are hard questions I've had to face. My situation shook my faith. It forced me to look deep inside my soul for answers.

The reality is—when everything else falls away, there is only trust. And sometimes, God allows circumstances to bring us to that point.

My close friends have been incredibly encouraging—calling, checking in, showing love. I've lost friends, too. But none of them can find my daughter. Most of them haven't experienced anything like this, so they don't have answers.

The best thing they've done is point me back to Christ—reminding me that He is real, He hears my prayers, and He sees my daughter.

I can't put all my trust in my counselor, even though they've been a lifeline in this chaos. They don't know where our daughter is either. She doesn't have a phone, so I can't trust that I can reach her. And I can't trust my pastor to have all the answers; he's human, too.

There was a time I pinned all my hope on a private detective. *This is it,* I thought. *This is his job—he'll find her.* I gave him everything I had—information, photos, notes—and he never responded to a single call or text. Can you imagine the desperation I felt being dismissed like that?

I still can't understand how a professional could do that to a grieving mother. It's another moment in this journey where I had to lay my anger before the Lord—or it would have destroyed me.

Another detective told me flat out: "It's extremely difficult to find people who don't want to be found."

So where do you go from there?

You go to God—who knows all things and truly loves His people.

Even if I never get the happy ending, I want—even if my daughter never comes home—I know God still loves me and will take care of every step I take.

But how am I behaving while I wait for His answer?

Sometimes, I admit, I get distracted. I search the internet for information. I latch onto advice from people who don't understand this situation. It's like I'm grasping for straws, trying to figure out how a child raised in a Christian home, filled with love and stability, could now be out on the streets doing things so opposite of how she was raised.

But when I focus each day on God's Word—when I truly believe that He cares for me and knows the plans He has for my life—I experience peace. I experience hope for my daughter. And I believe that for you too.

I imagine you reading these words, and I want you to know: If your child never comes home (as I know some of you reading this have experienced), I fully trust God will walk beside me—and beside you—through the darkest of days.

~hindsight helping tips~

· · · · ·

✎ When I feel overwhelmed with anxiety about our daughter, I picture myself walking down a mountain, carrying her in my arms, and placing her on an altar for Jesus to care for. Just like Abraham did with Isaac. That image brings me peace as I walk away knowing *God has got this.*

✎ I read verses about trusting God—morning and night. Memorizing Scripture has become essential for me.

✎ Sometimes I simply pray, "Lord, have mercy," over and over until I feel peace. Those three words cover it all.

✎ At times, I lay on the floor in a star shape—arms and legs outstretched—and tell God, "I surrender." It's one of the most freeing things I've ever done.

NOTES: _____

_____

_____

_____

_____

_____

_____

"So where do you go from there?

You go to God— who knows all things and truly loves His people."

Shout for joy, you heavens;
rejoice, you earth;
burst into song, you mountains!
For the Lord comforts his people
and will have compassion on his afflicted ones.
— Isaiah 49:13 (NIV)

• • • •

~chapter ten~ 🌸

SIBLINGS OF ADDICTS

THIS IS A TOUGH CHAPTER THAT TRULY BREAKS MY HEART. WE have two additional children—both adopted, now in their 20s—who have been loving, kind, and compliant from day one. They've faced challenges of their own due to prenatal exposure to drugs, but they've always been grateful, resilient, and eager to learn and grow. Their lives have been a blessing to us.

Just within the last few years, both of them have begun to express—in counseling and in conversations with us—the deep pain they experienced growing up alongside their older sister. Thankfully, she was never physically abusive, but there was a clear issue of control and emotional distress.

I should have seen the signs as early as age five. I remember walking into the room and seeing her playing with a toy phone. I asked, "Oh, are you talking to Grandma?" She looked at me and replied, "No. I'm talking to President Bush." She was five years old. I ran to my journal and wrote those words down because I thought it was so cute. I even thought, *"She's going to be a successful CEO one day."* And I do believe God gave her strong leadership qualities—but any gift can be used in the wrong direction.

According to our other children, she was cruel and manipulative when we weren't around. She would say hurtful, hateful things to them like, *God doesn't really love you.* It was so damaging that both of them have needed counseling to process the trauma. And it wasn't just the emotional abuse—it was the constant disruption. The chaos. The yelling. The unpredictability.

They would often retreat together to our middle daughter's room, just waiting for the storm to pass. They had to watch me fall apart, over and over again. They saw me cry. They saw me broken. And that hurt them too.

Of course, we had many beautiful family moments—but some of our vacations had to be cut short because our oldest daughter would misbehave, pushing everyone's buttons until we simply couldn't go on.

We were constantly in need of breaks. Thankfully, we had a cabin at the time. That place became a lifeline. We took turns—bringing each child up there one-on-one, giving the other parent time to regroup and rebuild strength. Those solo retreats were our way of providing space and care—for them, and for us.

hindsight helping tips

......

- Remember the other children in your home are also grieving. They're experiencing their own kind of loss, pain, and abandonment—even if they don't say it out loud.

- Make intentional efforts to spend time with your other children—just the two of you, or with your spouse. Take them on short trips, to lunch, or simply out for a drive. They need your undivided attention, too.

- Family therapy is a powerful tool. It gives everyone—especially the siblings—a safe space to express how the family dynamic has affected them. It also helps the child causing the disruptions to see the broader impact of their actions.

- Isaiah 49:13 – "Shout for joy, you heavens; rejoice, you earth; burst into song, you mountains! For the Lord comforts His people and will have compassion on His afflicted ones."

NOTES: _____

_____

_____

_____

_____

_____

But when you pray, go into your room, close the door and pray to your Father, who is unseen. Then your Father, who sees what is done in secret, will reward you.
— Matthew 6:6 (NIV)

chapter eleven

BIZARRE STORY ON THE POWER OF PRAYER

I WANT TO END THIS BOOK WITH A POSITIVE STORY ABOUT THE power of prayer in my life. I pray it encourages you to remember that God is bigger and stronger than we can imagine. We may think we're praying for one thing, while God is working behind the scenes—changing hearts, transforming lives.

Stacked in my closet are journals nearly three feet high, and many of them bear the name of a man I've never met—a man I prayed for faithfully for over 20 years. I believed he had gone to jail for drug use. What I would later discover was far more than I ever anticipated.

Twenty-six years ago, my husband and I adopted our first child—a baby girl. We knew her birth father had gone to jail, but we didn't think much about it. Her birth mother was unable to care for her. We bonded immediately with this child, and she was the answer to our prayers.

When our daughter was just a week old, we received a call that her birthfather had escaped from jail. That's when I wrote his name in my journal for the first time—under the section labeled *"Prayer Requests."* The police found him a week later. And so the prayers continued. As did his life of crime.

Fast forward 22 years.

It was a quiet, rainy evening in December 2020. I was reading my Bible and praying when I felt prompted—strongly—to open my laptop and search the birth father's name.

What I found stunned me. A local news anchor had interviewed him. I clicked play and watched in awe.

His body was covered in tattoos—from his Adam's apple down to his forearms. He shared his story: he had once led the largest white supremacist gang in our state. He had been arrested more than 70 times and charged with multiple felonies, including taking a life.

My heart began to race.

Then the anchor asked, "What changed you?"

He said a fellow prisoner asked him if he was ready to accept Christ. He said yes.

Everything changed.

He began leading others in prison to Christ and teaching Bible studies.

After serving a 20-year sentence, he was now working at a Christian rehabilitation center for ex-convicts in our state.

Shaking, tears streaming down my face, I picked up the phone and called the facility. For the first time in my life, I spoke to my daughter's birth father.

I told him, through sobs, that I had prayed for his salvation for 22 years.

He was in shock.

He thanked me over and over again.

We agreed to meet.

My husband wasn't ready for that meeting, so I went alone.

I wasn't afraid—but I was very anxious.

Driving to the facility, I kept wondering: *What if he thinks I'm crazy? What if he's not kind to me?*

But I had to go. I had something important to share—and I was hoping he might be able to help.

When I arrived and signed in at the front desk, it felt like I was meeting a dignitary. People whispered that I was there to see him.

There I was in my jean dress, tapping my feet in anticipation.

He walked around the corner, smiled, and gave me a huge hug. His tattoos were as visible as they were on the video. He was tall— like my daughter—and had the same hazel eyes.

He addressed the room: "This is Dena. We share a daughter together." I smiled and stood still. Next, he introduced me to the staff, each with their own story of transformation. Finally, he led me into a room with five older men—all dressed in black suits.

Every one of them was an ex-convict.

One had served 35 years. Another, 25.

An elderly man—about 75 years old—shuffled in with a cane and said, "So this is Dena." He had once been on death row. Now, he was leading inmates to Christ.

He told me that my faithful prayers had played a role in stopping evil in our state—through the radical transformation of my daughter's birth father. He said hundreds had come to Christ because of that man's prison outreach. I felt an avalanche of tears rising within me. The power of prayer. I was thankful to see all that God was doing in their lives

Later, I had some one-on-one time with my daughter's birth father. I had difficult news to share. I told him we had tried to raise our daughter with morals, Christian values, and a strong education. But she had been a defiant child from the start, and eventually left home to pursue a life of addiction.

For years, we'd received late-night phone calls and unexpected visits from strangers showing up at our house with her. The chaos became constant. Hundreds of sleepless nights. And now, six years without seeing her. She's missing.

He looked me in the eyes and thanked me again for my prayers—saying they had radically changed his life. He reminded me that God *does* hear our prayers. I looked back into his eyes and asked for his forgiveness.

Even though I had prayed for him faithfully, I'd also harbored bitterness—for all the pain we had endured raising his child, who became our child. I wanted an apology from him, but I didn't receive one. Still—God used my obedience in offering forgiveness to set me free.

We've kept in touch over the last few years. He often reminds me of the truth found in God's Word: God is still in control. He also reminded me that I never reached out to him during the 20 years in prison, yet God heard my prayers. And right now I can't connect to my daughter either—so I continue to pray.

When I think about all those years of faithfully praying for his soul, I feel renewed confidence that God is also hearing my daily prayers for our daughter.

hindsight helping tips

· · ● ● ·

- ❧ Never stop praying for your situation. Even if you hear nothing for years, trust that God is working behind the scenes.

- ❧ Recognize that God is bigger than you. You don't have control—and your human mind can't comprehend all that He's orchestrating.

- ❧ Know that God desires your trust and obedience. He holds the answers. And even when things don't go the way we hope, He will walk closely beside us.

- ❧ Step outside your pain and make a difference somewhere else while you wait. Serve. Create. Encourage. Your story isn't on pause.

- ❧ You can carry heartache and still touch others with your gifts, love, and joy. I couldn't believe this six years ago, but now I know it's true. I strive to spread goodness—even while carrying grief. It's possible.

- ❧ Matthew 6:6 – "But when you pray, go into your room and shut the door and pray to your Father who is in secret. And your Father who sees in secret will reward you."

NOTES: _____

_____

_____

_____

CONCLUSION

MY DESIRE FOR THIS BOOK WAS TO BE AN ENCOURAGEMENT TO those walking the road of utter desperation and deep sadness—offering even the smallest thread of hope. Maybe you're not facing addiction in your life, but you've been praying for something for years—still waiting for an answer.

I wanted this book to be shorter in length because I've noticed that most people either don't have the time—or the desire—to read a 300-page book. My hope is that this can serve as a reference guide, a source of inspiration, and a nudge to help you get off the couch of anguish and step back into the game of life.

People still need you.

Our loved ones have choices to make, and we can't control them. I remind myself of this often, as I am the self-proclaimed President of the Controlling Mothers Club—if there ever were such an organization.

As I'm typing these final words, I'm thinking about you—the person who took the time to read my story of heartache and hope. Thank you. It's hard to put yourself out there on paper—to expose your deepest wounds.

But what if more people did that? What if we shared the real, raw parts of our journeys—not just the polished highlights? Could that vulnerability lower suicide rates? Maybe.

When I listen to a speaker, a sermon, or read a book, I'm not looking for perfect answers or a five-step path to success. I want to hear about the hard places—the places that required grit, faith, and daily courage just to get out of bed. That, in my opinion, is where healing begins. That's what touches people's hearts.

I remember being in grade school, sitting at a picnic table at recess with the popular girls. I looked over and saw a blonde-haired girl sitting alone. My heart hurt. So, I left the table and went to sit with her, even as the others asked why I would leave *their* table to sit with *her*.

That moment shaped something in me. It became a pattern in my life—to seek out the brokenhearted. If your heart is shattered right now, have courage. Be brave. You are not alone. And with God, all things are possible. 2 Corinthians 5:7 — *"For we live by faith, not by sight."* There is always hope in God, in *every* circumstance.

Every day, I still pray in hope that our daughter will lift her eyes to heaven and realize she is loved—not just by me, but far more than that—by God Himself.

So if the blueprint you drew for your life didn't match the one that unfolded—it's okay. God is the ultimate architect. He can rebuild. He can make all things new—if you let Him.

Stay brave. Know that others are walking through battles like yours. We can still create a beautiful life for ourselves and the world around us—even in the middle of heartbreak.

Sending love your way.

ABOUT THE AUTHOR

DENA L. WALL IS THE AUTHOR OF *YOU CAN LIVE BRAVE,* HER latest work of heartfelt insight and inspiration, as well as *Simple Surprises: The Art of Encouragement and Creative Gift Giving,* and numerous magazine articles.

She holds degrees in Public Relations and Business Management, and brings a thoughtful, real-world perspective to her writing.

Dena is the mother of three grown children and shares life's journey with her husband, Kevin, a chiropractic physician and co-owner of several health clinics in Arizona.

Contact the author at: youcanlivebrave@gmail.com

www.ingramcontent.com/pod-product-compliance
Lightning Source LLC
Chambersburg PA
CBHW051704090426
42736CB00013B/2525